DISCOVERING THE BEAUTY OF A PARROTFISH

Do Your Kids Know This?

A Children's Picture Book
Amazing Creature Series

Tanya Turner

PUBLISHED BY:

Tanya Turner

Copyright © 2016

TABLE OF CONTENTS

The Parrotfish 5

Getting to Know the Parrotfish 6

Mucus Defense 8

The Feeding Activity of the Parrotfish 9

Life Cycle of a Parrotfish 13

Where Can You Find a Parrotfish? 15

Predators of a Parrotfish 16

Parrotfish as a Pet 18

The Parrotfish

The parrotfish.

Is it a bird? Or is it a fish? Well, the parrotfish is actually a fish.

Yes, it's a fish with some characteristics of the parrot bird – that's why it's called a parrotfish. You can already tell that it's going to be fun to learn more about this unique and amazing creature of the sea. So let's get started, shall we?

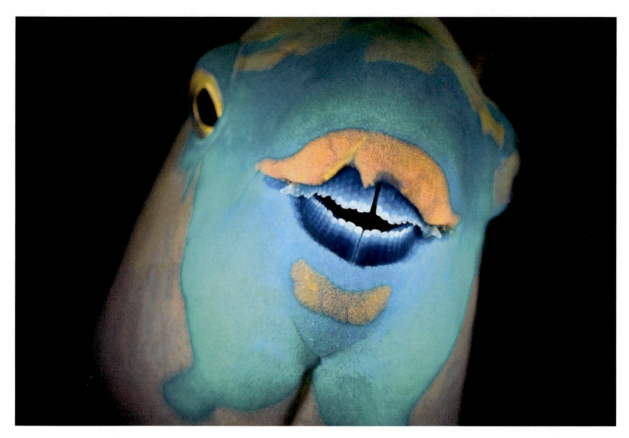
Face to face with a parrotfish.

Getting to Know the Parrotfish

The parrotfish is a type of fish with thick bodies and big scales. Their sizes vary, and you can find some which are small – only about 13 cm. There are also large types of parrotfish which can be as big as 4 feet or more – that's almost the size of a child! Wow!

In addition, there are also those which are medium sized, about 1 to 2 feet – which is still quite big compared to the ordinary types of fish (especially those that are kept in aquariums).

The parrotfish mainly got its name for the formation of its teeth. The teeth in their mouths are arranged in such a unique way that no other fish has. To be more specific, their teeth are tightly arranged and packed along their jawbones to make their mouths seem like a bird's beak. In particular, their mouth is formed like a parrot's beak.

Nature didn't design the parrotfish this way for no reason. The mouths of this particular fish can chew on rocks and corals found under the sea. They actually don't eat rocks and corals, but the plants and algae that are attached on the surfaces of these structures.

The process of eating up corals is called Bioerosion. This process leads to the formation of sands under the water. So you see, the Parrotfish also contributes to the preservation and maintenance of the seas.

A parrotfish displaying its colorful scales.

Mucus Defense

Another interesting characteristic of the parrotfish is its mucus defense system. This type of fish has the ability to release a slimy substance to cover itself for protection. It's like a blanket that can cover the whole fish up.

They usually use their mucus defense at night when they go to sleep. Remember, a lot of other creatures are present in the water, and a lot of these creatures are hunting for food at night. So, in order to protect itself from being eaten or attacked by other sea creatures, the parrotfish hides itself in a mucus blanket before going to sleep. The covering will not only cover the fish itself but its scent too.

A parrotfish eating microorganisms among corals.

Since the mucus blanket can make the Parrotfish seem invisible to some creatures of the sea, it can keep the fish safe. However, there are also other sea animals with good senses of sight and smell, that they can spot a parrotfish even if it's covered in a mucus blanket.

The mucus covering can also serve as a means to delay attackers. When the Parrotfish senses something trying to destroy its mucus membrane covering, it can wake up and swim away from the attacker.

The Feeding Activity of the Parrotfish

The parrotfish has a very interesting feeding activity because of their teeth. This type of fish is actually categorized as detritivores, which means that they feed on a wide variety of microorganisms in the water – basically every living thing attached on corals and the surface of the sands.

A group of green humphead parrotfishes swimming among corals.

Their actual feeding activity – the scratching and munching on the surfaces of corals and rock formations, aids in the formation and distribution of sands under the water. Their eating style also prevents algae and other types of plants from growing uncontrollably under the sea. Now, this is really important as too much plant growth can also cause pollution in the water when they deteriorate and die. That's why it's also important to have plant eating creatures under the sea to maintain the natural balance in the underwater world.

A parrotfish has really strong teeth to munch on corals.

Without dentists under the sea, how can a parrotfish maintain healthy teeth? Well, nature has taken care of this problem too, as the teeth of the parrotfish are continually growing. So, while you can expect their teeth to wear out because of the constant chewing and grinding on hard surfaces, the continuous growth of their teeth will naturally replace the parts that have been worn out or broken.

Keep in mind, however, that parrotfish only eat the plants and microorganisms present on the surfaces of rocks and corals. So while they are able to eat parts of the hard surfaces, their bodies are not able to digest these as food. After entering their bodies, only the food particles are digested and absorbed by the fish – and the undigested substances, the particles of corals and rocks are released from their bodies in the form of sand. In short, their poop contains sand particles that go back into the sea.

Different species of parrotfish can be found all over the world.

Now, there's a particular type of parrotfish that can produce a lot of sand – it's called the Green Humphead. This is a big type of parrotfish, and it has been estimated that it can produce about 200 pounds of sand every year – just by its eating habits.

This type of fish really plays a huge part in sustaining the presence of sand underwater, which is important in maintaining healthy bodies of water. It's quite hard to break down the amount of sand each type of parrotfish can produce, because they come in different varieties and sizes and are present in different places in the world. All in all, however, it has been estimated that the average sand production of each parrotfish in the world is about 275 grams per fish, per day. That's still a lot.

A school of parrotfish hunting for food.

Life Cycle of a Parrotfish

Just as the parrotfish has a unique appearance and special eating habits, it also has a complicated and interesting life cycle. Its development itself is again different from other types of fish, as its colors can change several times throughout its life.

Most types of parrotfish are called Hermaphrodites. This means that parrotfishes can change its classification of sex at least once in its lifetime. In fact, it can do so, again and again.

Yes, you may find it hard to believe, but a male parrotfish can change into a female fish just as a female parrotfish can change into a male fish. It can also happen that a baby parrotfish is born male but will mature into a female fish. There's really no pattern for the change in sex – it just happens. To this date, there is only one type of parrotfish that is not known to change its sex – the marbled parrotfish.

Just look at those teeth!

As for breeding, a parrotfish lays eggs just like any other types of fish. It can lay many small eggs that are quite light. These eggs will float freely under the water as the mother fish lays her eggs. Soon enough, these eggs will settle among the corals and sands under the sea.

Needless to say, it would be safer for the eggs to land somewhere where they are not exposed to danger. Remember, the sea is full of scavengers and hunters, and exposed eggs can be eaten by sea creatures looking for food.

Fortunately, parrotfish eggs are just so many that a lot of their babies survive to adulthood. Keep in mind, too, that this type of fish has the mucus defense strategy - that helps in keeping themselves protected too. And because of all the factors that make up the life cycle of the parrotfish, they are expected to live up to 20 years.

A parrotfish resting under the sea.

Can you imagine how many parrotfish babies can be born in those 20 years? That'll be lots and lots of babies! And as the parrotfish babies mature, they will be able to have their own eggs and babies too, right? This life cycle will just go on and on and on to keep the population of parrotfish thriving in the seas.

Moreover, parrotfishes can also have their own colonies or families. Groups of fish are also called schools of fish – so there's such a thing as a school of parrotfish. This group typically has one male and about ten females. As the leader of the group, the male will guard their home in the sea and protect it from enemies (other creatures of the sea) and other types of fish as well.

Where Can You Find a Parrotfish?

Fortunately, parrotfishes can be seen all over the world – so, they are not hard to find. However, you can find them in great abundance among tropical reefs where the water is not that cold.

As with other types of fish, parrotfish also prefers living in clean waters. You will rarely find fish in polluted areas because aquatic animals simply can't tolerate such environments. If humans are greatly affected by air pollution, the fish in the sea are affected by water pollution. The reason for this is that fish breathe under the water too, just as people breathe in air.

Having different species of parrotfish helps in the formation of sand.

Polluted waters also can't provide food for sea animals. And parrotfishes, in particular, eat microorganisms and plants found in the bottom of the sea. And with polluted waters, even plants and microorganisms will die. So in cases like this, sea animals will leave places that are polluted and find places where they can live and eat without pollution.

Predators of a Parrotfish

Not all underwater creatures live in harmony. While some types of sea creatures live peacefully, some are simply vicious animals. It's actually a natural thing under the sea, as these animals need to eat in order to survive.

A parrotfish is more active at night as it sleeps during the day.

So while groups of parrotfishes are quite friendly with one another, they are careful with other types of creatures living under the sea with them. Big types of fish can actually attack and eat them, especially those types of Parrotfish that are quite small. The eggs are also in danger of being eaten by swimming and crawling sea animals like crabs and shrimps as the eggs are simply settled on sands, plants and rocks.

Of course, as a parrotfish matures, its chances for survival also increase. Not only can a parrotfish use its mucus defense system, it can also swim faster to get away from its enemies.

The parrotfish really needs to be brave and strong to survive life under the sea because there are big and small creatures that can be dangerous to them. Just think about eels, snakes, and sharks – all these scary sea animals can easily kill a parrotfish. After all, it doesn't have any special skills or weapons to fight back its enemies.

The mouth of a Parrotfish looks like a parrot's beak.

Parrotfish as a Pet

A parrotfish is actually one of the most popular types of fish for aquariums. This is mainly because of their looks, of course.

Since this type of fish somewhat looks like a bird (a parrot, in particular), it's really interesting to see it swimming in water. That alone makes it an interesting aquarium pet.

A Parrotfish swimming with other sea creatures.

Aside from their cute and unique shape, this type of fish is also colorful and lively. They have bright colored scales that are simply beautiful.

Devoted parrotfish owners are also amazed by the personality of this particular fish. According to some pet fish owners, the parrotfish can recognize people and even form bond with humans. This can be observed as a parrotfish come near the sides of the aquarium when it sees its owner or the person that usually feeds it. So, it's quite like owning other types of pets too – they become close to the person responsible for feeding them.

Is it practical to have a parrotfish as a pet? Well, as with all pets, you need to make a lot of preparations when considering getting a pet parrotfish. For one, know that this type of fish can grow big, so you need a big aquarium for this, especially if you plan on owning more than one.

This Parrotfish looks like its smiling.

Furthermore, you have to consider the eating habits of the parrotfish too. If you have corals and rocks as decorations in your aquarium, expect these to eventually be eaten away by the fish. And of course, you also need to clean the aquarium regularly, so as to provide a clean environment for your pet fish.

Are you up to the task? If you are, your new best friend could be a parrotfish.

Images from:

Rich Carey, Levent Konuk, wittaya changkaew, LauraD, Nick Utchin, sergemi, Vilainecrevette, Zoonar GmbH, Joe Quinn, aquapix, SeraphP, wittaya changkaew/Shutterstock.com

Disclaimer

The information contained in this book is for general information purposes only. The information is provided by the authors and, while we endeavor to keep the information up to date and correct, we make no representations or warranties of any kind, expressed or implied, about the completeness, accuracy, reliability, suitability or availability with respect to the book or the information, products, services, or related graphics contained in the book for any purpose. Any reliance you place on such information is therefore strictly at your own risk.

Made in the USA
Monee, IL
16 April 2024